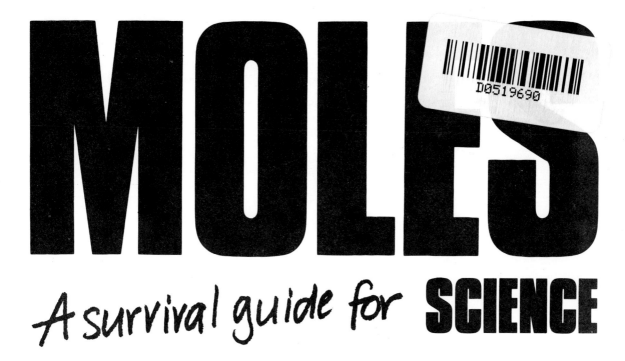

MOLES
A survival guide for SCIENCE

KEITH BROWN
BTech (Hons), MSc

Deputy Headteacher
Bewdley High School,
Bewdley, Worcestershire

CAMBRIDGE
UNIVERSITY PRESS

Published by the Press Syndicate of the University of Cambridge
The Pitt Building, Trumpington Street, Cambridge CB2 1RP
40 West 20th Street, New York, NY 10011–4211, USA
10 Stamford Road, Oakleigh, Victoria 3166, Australia

First published as *Moles: a survival guide for GCSE Chemistry* 1986
Fifth printing 1989
Second edition *Moles: a survival guide for GCSE Science* 1991
Reprinted as *Moles: a survival guide for Science* 1992

Printed in Great Britain by Scotprint Ltd., Musselburgh

A catalogue record for this book is available from the British Library

ISBN 0 521 42409 7

Acknowledgements

The exercises and approach used in this book were developed with the
help of staff and Year Eleven pupils at Archbishop Ilsley School and
Bewdley High School. I am particularly indebited to Caroline Willmot,
Richard Caddick, Stuart Morris, Steven Moss, Leon O'Malley and Tim
Shepherd who corrected my many and varied errors.

Acknowledgement is made to the *Daily Mirror* (© Syndication
International) and to the *Daily Mail* for kindly giving permission to
incorporate the 'Perishers' and 'Fred Basset' cartoons. The Midland
Examining Group gave permission to use The Periodic Table of Elements
shown on page 4.

CONTENTS

The Periodic Table of the Elements

Group I	II										III	IV	V	VI	VII	0
						1 **H** Hydrogen 1										4 **He** Helium 2
7 **Li** Lithium 3	9 **Be** Beryllium 4										11 **B** Boron 5	12 **C** Carbon 6	14 **N** Nitrogen 7	16 **O** Oxygen 8	19 **F** Fluorine 9	20 **Ne** Neon 10
23 **Na** Sodium 11	24 **Mg** Magnesium 12										27 **Al** Aluminium 13	28 **Si** Silicon 14	31 **P** Phosphorus 15	32 **S** Sulphur 16	35.5 **Cl** Chlorine 17	40 **Ar** Argon 18
39 **K** Potassium 19	40 **Ca** Calcium 20	45 **Sc** Scandium 21	48 **Ti** Titanium 22	51 **V** Vanadium 23	52 **Cr** Chromium 24	55 **Mn** Manganese 25	56 **Fe** Iron 26	59 **Co** Cobalt 27	59 **Ni** Nickel 28	64 **Cu** Copper 29	65 **Zn** Zinc 30	70 **Ga** Gallium 31	73 **Ge** Germanium 32	75 **As** Arsenic 33	79 **Se** Selenium 34	80 **Br** Bromine 35
85 **Rb** Rubidium 37	88 **Sr** Strontium 38	89 **Y** Yttrium 39	91 **Zr** Zirconium 40	93 **Nb** Niobium 41	96 **Mo** Molybdenum 42	**Tc** Technetium 43	101 **Ru** Ruthenium 44	103 **Rh** Rhodium 45	106 **Pd** Palladium 46	108 **Ag** Silver 47	112 **Cd** Cadmium 48	115 **In** Indium 49	119 **Sn** Tin 50	122 **Sb** Antimony 51	128 **Te** Tellurium 52	127 **I** Iodine 53
133 **Cs** Caesium 55	137 **Ba** Barium 56	139 **La** Lanthanum 57 *	178 **Hf** Hafnium 72	181 **Ta** Tantalum 73	184 **W** Tungsten 74	186 **Re** Rhenium 75	190 **Os** Osmium 76	192 **Ir** Iridium 77	195 **Pt** Platinum 78	197 **Au** Gold 79	201 **Hg** Mercury 80	204 **Tl** Thallium 81	207 **Pb** Lead 82	209 **Bi** Bismuth 83	**Po** Polonium 84	**At** Astatine 85
Fr Francium 87	226 **Ra** Radium 88	227 **Ac** Actinium 89 †														**Rn** Radon 86

Xenon															
131 **Xe** 54															
175 **Lu** Lutetium 71															
173 **Yb** Ytterbium 70															
169 **Tm** Thulium 69															

Lanthanum series

140 **Ce** Cerium 58	141 **Pr** Praseodymium 59	144 **Nd** Neodymium 60	**Pm** Promethium 61	150 **Sm** Samarium 62	152 **Eu** Europium 63	157 **Gd** Gadolinium 64	159 **Tb** Terbium 65	162 **Dy** Dysprosium 66	165 **Ho** Holmium 67	167 **Er** Erbium 68	169 **Tm** Thulium 69	173 **Yb** Ytterbium 70	175 **Lu** Lutetium 71

Actinium series

232 **Th** Thorium 90	**Pa** Protactinium 91	238 **U** Uranium 92	**Np** Neptunium 93	**Pu** Plutonium 94	**Am** Americium 95	**Cm** Curium 96	**Bk** Berkelium 97	**Cf** Californium 98	**Es** Einsteinium 99	**Fm** Fermium 100	**Md** Mendelevium 101	**No** Nobelium 102	**Lr** Lawrencium 103

* 58-71 Lanthanum series
† 90-103 Actinium series

Key

$$a = \text{relative atomic mass}$$
$$\text{X} = \text{atomic symbol}$$
$$b = \text{atomic number}$$

$$\text{number of moles of atoms} = \frac{\text{mass of element/g}}{\text{relative atomic mass } (A_r)}$$

$$\text{number of moles of substance} = \frac{\text{mass of substance/g}}{\text{relative molecular mass } (M_r)}$$

The volume of one mole of any gas is $24\,\text{dm}^3$ (litres) at room temperature and pressure (r.t.p.).

MOLE 1 | LET'S START AT THE VERY BEGINNING

Atoms are very small indeed! If we drew a line 1 metre long, 6 000 000 000 (6 billion) atoms could be lined end to end.

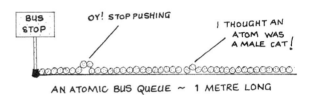

BUS STOP

OY! STOP PUSHING

I THOUGHT AN ATOM WAS A MALE CAT!

AN ATOMIC BUS QUEUE ~ 1 METRE LONG

So a scientist cannot count atoms, ions or molecules directly. They are far too small and numerous. Instead she counts particles by **weighing**. This is rather like in a bank. A bank cashier has not got the time to count every coin. She weighs the bags of coins on special scales which tell her how much they are worth.

ELECTRON MOVING AROUND THE NUCLEUS

The lightest atom is **hydrogen**. Hydrogen has got just **one proton** and **one electron**.

NUCLEUS CONTAINING A SINGLE PROTON

Since hydrogen is the lightest atom, we say that hydrogen has a **relative atomic mass** of **1**. Even in 1 g of hydrogen there are an awful lot of atoms. In 1 g of hydrogen atoms we say that we have **one mole** of atoms.

YOU CALLED?

Experiments have shown that an atom of **carbon** weighs **12 times** as much as an atom of hydrogen. So the **relative atomic mass** of carbon is **12**. Relative atomic mass can be shorted to A_r.

Now put your thinking cap on

If a scientist weighed out 1 g of hydrogen atoms and wished to have an **equal** number of carbon atoms, she would need to weigh out **12 g** of carbon atoms. In 12 g of carbon there will also be **one mole** of atoms.

Let us take another example. A **lead** atom is **207 times** heavier than a hydrogen atom. The **relative atomic mass** of lead must be **207**. If a scientist weighed out 207 g of lead atoms she would have **one mole** of atoms. In 207 g of lead there are exactly the same number of atoms as there are in 12 g of carbon.

We can use this idea of weighing to include any element.

YOU CALLED?

Look at your Periodic Table

Spot sodium and magnesium. Make a note of their relative atomic masses.

You see that sodium has a relative atomic mass of **23**. If a scientist weighed out **23 g** of sodium she would have **one mole** of sodium atoms. Magnesium has a relative atomic mass of **24**. If a scientist wanted to have **one mole** of magnesium atoms, she would weigh out **24 g**.

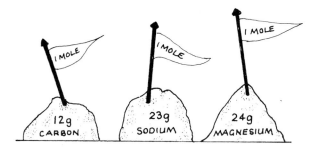

IN EACH PILE THERE IS ONE MOLE OF ATOMS

Exercise 1.1

Use your copy of the Periodic Table to find out the mass of one mole of the following atoms.

(*a*) Helium   (*b*) Iron   (*c*) Potassium   (*d*) Sulphur
(*e*) Platinum   (*f*) Tin   (*g*) Iodine   (*h*) Phosphorus

How many atoms are there in one mole?

We have learned that one mole of any element contains the same number of atoms. This is such a large number it is almost impossible to imagine. Far more than there are people on the Earth!

One mole is about 6×10^{23} atoms. Six times 10 to the power 23.

COUNT 'EM!

6×10

This scientific 'magic number' is called **Avogadro's number** or **Avogadro's constant**.

6

When we are dealing with fractions or multiples of 6×10^{23} we must remember to alter the '6' part only. Do **not** alter the '10^{23}' part unless you know what you are doing!

For example half of 6×10^{23} is 3×10^{23}.
Five times 6×10^{23} is 30×10^{23}.
(Actually this answer is also equal to 3×10^{24}!)

The word Avogadro is in honour of Amedeo Avogadro. He was a famous nineteenth-century Italian chemist.

Example One

How many atoms are there in 6 g of carbon?

Answer

The relative atomic mass of carbon is 12. In 12 g of carbon there are 6×10^{23} atoms which is one mole. In 6 g of carbon there is half a mole, which is **3×10^{23} atoms**.

Exercise 1.2

Use your copy of the Periodic Table to help you. How many atoms are there in

(a) 39 g potassium, (b) 2 g helium, (c) 54 g aluminium,
(d) 54 g silver, (e) 119 g tin, (f) 6 g carbon,
(g) 112 g iron, (h) 8 g sulphur?

What we have learned in

MOLE 1

(1) Scientists count atoms, ions and molecules by weighing.
(2) If the relative atomic mass of an element is weighed out in grams, then one mole of atoms is present.
(3) One mole of atoms is about 6×10^{23} atoms.
(4) 6×10^{23} is called Avogadro's number or Avogadro's constant.

MOLE 2

CONVERTING MASSES INTO MOLES – AND MOLES INTO MASSES

In everyday life a scientist rarely measures atoms, ions or molecules in whole moles. He will have a fraction of a mole or several moles. Luckily it is easy to turn the mass of an element into moles by using one simple equation.

$$\text{Number of moles} = \frac{\text{mass of element}}{\text{relative atomic mass of element}}$$

Learn this

Example One

How many moles of atoms are there in 4 g of calcium?
[A_r (Ca) = 40]

Answer

$$\text{Number of moles} = \frac{\text{mass of element}}{\text{relative atomic mass of element}} = \frac{4}{40} = \frac{1}{10} \text{ mole or } \textbf{0.1 mole}.$$

By rearranging the equation it is just as easy to find out the mass of a fraction of a mole. Does that sound confusing? Look at Example Two.

Example Two

What is the mass of $\frac{1}{8}$ of a mole of copper?

[A_r (Cu) = 64]

Answer

First our equation must be rearranged:

mass = number of moles × relative atomic mass

$\text{mass} = \frac{1}{8} \times 64 = \textbf{8 g}$ (Don't forget the units!).

Exercise 2.1 (These are the easy questions Your relative atomic masses are shown on the right-hand side.)

How many moles of atoms are there in

(a) 20 g calcium, (b) 54 g aluminium, (c) 11.2 g iron,
(d) 78 g potassium, (e) 8 g sulphur, (f) 2.4 g magnesium?

What is the mass of

(g) $\frac{1}{10}$ mole of sodium atoms, (h) 2 moles of silver atoms,
(i) $\frac{1}{3}$ mole of carbon atoms, (j) 8 moles of iron atoms,
(k) $\frac{1}{16}$ mole of magnesium (l) $\frac{1}{4}$ mole of copper atoms?
                atoms,

Exercise 2.2 (OK Here are the creep point questions. Again the relative atomic masses are on the right-hand side.)

Avogadro's number $= 6 \times 10^{23}$

Relative atomic masses		
Ag	=	108
Al	=	27
C	=	12
Ca	=	40
Cu	=	64
Fe	=	56
K	=	39
Mg	=	24
Na	=	23
S	=	32
O	=	16
Pb	=	207

How many atoms are there in

(a) 1 mole of carbon atoms, (b) 2 moles of oxygen atoms,
(c) $\frac{1}{2}$ mole of sulphur atoms, (d) $\frac{1}{3}$ mole of lead atoms?
(e) What mass of magnesium contains 2×10^{23} atoms?
(f) What mass of carbon contains 2×10^{23} atoms?
(g) What mass of magnesium has five times as many atoms as 2 g of carbon?
(h) What mass of potassium has the same number of atoms as 8 g of magnesium?

What we have learned in

MOLE 2

(1) Scientists are not often able to work with one mole. They usually have fractions or multiples of a mole.
(2) To convert a given mass into moles we use:

$$\text{number of moles} = \frac{\text{mass of element}}{\text{relative atomic mass of element}}.$$

(3) To convert a number of moles into a mass we use:

$$\text{mass of element} = \text{number of moles} \times \text{relative atomic mass of element}.$$

MOLE 3

DIATOMIC MOLECULES

Sometimes an element exists as **molecules**. Molecules are groups of atoms held together by **chemical bonds**.

A molecule can be given a **formula**. The formula tells us which atoms are present. It also tells us how many atoms are present, joined together by chemical bonds.

A **diatomic molecule** contains two atoms. Elements which are gases at room temperature and pressure are often diatomic. For example hydrogen gas is made up of two hydrogen atoms in each molecule. It has the formula H_2. The formula of chlorine gas is Cl_2 and nitrogen gas has the formula N_2.

Thinking cap on again!

We must be careful when we are weighing moles of molecules.

A hydrogen atom has a relative atomic mass of 1. A hydrogen gas molecule has two atoms. If each atom has a relative atomic mass of 1, then the **relative molecular mass (M_r)** of the molecule is 2.

To have one mole of molecules we would need to weigh out 2 g of hydrogen gas. In one mole of molecules there will be 6×10^{23} molecules (Avogadro's number). We can use a similar equation to the one we met in Mole 2 to work out the number of moles of molecules.

$$\text{Number of moles} = \frac{\text{mass}}{\text{relative molecular mass}}$$

Relative molecular mass is sometimes called relative formula mass.

Example One

How many moles of nitrogen are present in 7 g of nitrogen gas? [A_r (N) = 14]

Answer

First note that the question did not ask about nitrogen atoms. It concerns nitrogen molecules, N_2. Each molecule contains two atoms of nitrogen. Since each atom has a relative atomic mass of 14, then nitrogen's relative molecular mass is $2 \times 14 = 28$.

$$\text{Number of moles} = \frac{\text{mass}}{\text{relative molecular mass}} = \frac{7}{28} = \frac{1}{4} \text{ mole or } \textbf{0.25 mole}.$$

Just like in Mole 2, we can rearrange the basic equation to convert a number of moles of a molecule into a mass. Confused again? Look at Example Two.

Example Two

What is the mass of $\frac{1}{10}$ mole of oxygen gas? [A_r (O) = 16]

Answer

Oxygen is a diatomic gas, O_2. It has the relative molecular mass $2 \times 16 = 32$. Now rearrange the basic formula:

$$\text{Mass} = \text{number of moles} \times \text{relative molecular mass} = \frac{1}{10} \times 32 = \textbf{3.2 g}.$$

Exercise 3.1

The relative atomic masses you need are on the right-hand side.

How many moles of

(a) chlorine are present in 7.1 g of chlorine gas,
(b) oxygen are present in 64 g of oxygen gas?

Exercise 3.2

The relative atomic masses you need are on the right-hand side.

What is the mass of

(a) $\frac{1}{8}$ mole of oxygen gas,   (b) $\frac{1}{4}$ mole of bromine gas,   (c) 2 moles of chlorine gas?

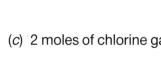

Relative atomic masses
Br = 80
Cl = 35.5
O = 16

What we have learned in

MOLE 3

(1) Some elements exist not as single atoms, but as molecules.
(2) A molecule contains two or more atoms joined by chemical bonds.
(3) A molecule can be given a formula to describe the number and type of atoms in it.
(4) To convert a given mass of molecules into moles we use:

$$\text{number of moles} = \frac{\text{mass}}{\text{relative molecular mass}}.$$

MOLE 4 COMPOUNDS

Some compounds are also made up of molecules. But a compound contains atoms of **different** elements joined together by chemical bonds.
The formula for water is H_2O. This means that a molecule of water contains two atoms of hydrogen and one atom of oxygen.

To work out the mass of **one mole** of a compound we use the same idea as in Mole 3. The relative atomic masses of **all** the atoms in the compound are added together.

Example One

What is the mass of one mole of water, H_2O?
$[A_r(H) = 1; A_r(O) = 16]$

MOLECULE OF WATER

H_2O

Answer

The water molecule contains two atoms of hydrogen and one atom of oxygen. The relative molecular mass of water is $(2 \times 1) + (1 \times 16) = $ **18**. The mass of one mole of water is **18 g**.

The relative molecular mass of a compound contains one mole of molecules. Hence in 18 g of water there are 6×10^{23} molecules of water.

When working out the relative molecular mass of a compound containing groups, such as nitrates, sulphates and carbonates, it is important to include every atom.

Example Two

What is the relative molecular mass of magnesium nitrate, $Mg(NO_3)_2$? $[A_r(Mg) = 24; A_r(N) = 14; A_r(O) = 16]$

Answer

Each mole of magnesium nitrate contains 1 mole of magnesium, 2 moles of nitrogen and 6 moles of oxygen. (**Think!** You have to double everything inside the brackets.)

So the relative molecular mass is $(1 \times 24) + (2 \times 14) + (6 \times 16) = 24 + 28 + 96 = 148$.

Exercise 4.1

The relative atomic masses you need are on the right-hand side.

Find the relative molecular mass of

(a) copper(II) oxide, CuO;
(b) sulphur trioxide, SO_3;
(c) copper(II) sulphide, CuS;
(d) copper(II) carbonate, $CuCO_3$;
(e) zinc nitrate, $Zn(NO_3)_2$;
(f) ammonium carbonate, $(NH_4)_2CO_3$.

To work out how many moles there are in a certain mass of a compound we use exactly the same formula that we met in Mole 3.

Relative atomic masses		
C	=	12
Cu	=	64
H	=	1
N	=	14
O	=	16
S	=	32
Zn	=	65

$$\text{Number of moles} = \frac{\text{mass}}{\text{relative molecular mass}}$$

Example Three

How many moles are contained in 72 g of water?

Answer

We have already found the relative molecular mass of water to be 18 in Example One.

So,

$$\text{number of moles} = \frac{\text{mass}}{\text{relative molecular mass}} = \frac{72}{18} = \textbf{4 moles}.$$

Exercise 4.2

The relative atomic masses you need are shown for Exercise 4.1.

Find the number of moles contained in

(a) 40 g copper(II) sulphate, $CuSO_4$;
(b) 282 g zinc carbonate, $ZnCO_3$;
(c) 60 g sulphur trioxide, SO_3;
(d) 32 g ammonium carbonate, $(NH_4)_2CO_3$.

If we want to convert a certain number of moles of a compound into an actual mass, then we rearrange the last equation.

Example Four

Find the mass of 0.2 mole of tetrachloromethane (carbon tetrachloride), CCl_4. [$A_r(C) = 12$; $A_r(Cl) = 35.5$]

Answer

The relative molecular mass of $CCl_4 = (1 \times 12) + (4 \times 35.5) = 154$.

Rearranging the last equation, we find

mass = number of moles × relative molecular mass = $0.2 \times 154 =$ **30.8 g**.

Exercise 4.3

The relative atomic masses you need are shown on the right-hand side.

Find the mass of

(a) 0.5 mole calcium carbonate, $CaCO_3$,
(b) ¼ mole copper(II) oxide, CuO,
(c) ⅟₁₀ mole of sulphur trioxide, SO_3,
(d) 0.25 mole ammonium carbonate, $(NH_4)_2CO_3$.

Relative atomic masses		
C	=	12
Ca	=	40
Cu	=	64
H	=	1
N	=	14
O	=	16
S	=	32

(1) Compounds are made up of molecules or giant structures that contain different elements.
(2) The relative molecular mass of a compound is found by adding together the relative atomic masses of each atom in the formula.
(3) To find out the number of moles in a certain mass of a compound we again use the equation:

$$\text{number of moles} = \frac{\text{mass}}{\text{relative molecular mass}}.$$

(4) To convert a certain number of moles into the mass of a compound, we rearrange the equation above:

mass = number of moles × relative molecular mass.

MOLE 5 GASES

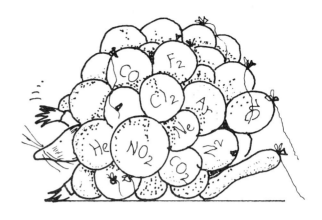

Gases can be difficult things to work with. They expand rapidly when they are heated. They contract easily when they are pressurised.

Gases are not very dense. The average pop bottle contains 1 litre of pop. One litre of air weighs just over 1 g!

So far in Moles 1–4 we have worked out moles by **weighing**. But obviously gases are going to be very difficult substances to weigh.

We can, however, measure the **volume** of gas quite easily, in a syringe or a graduated tube, or an inverted measuring cylinder.

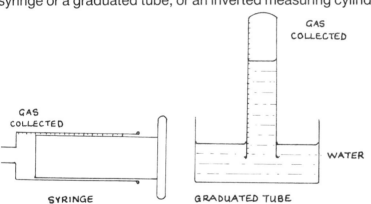

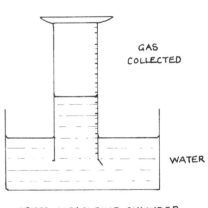

We are now on the right tracks because **all** gases have a strange property.

AT THE SAME TEMPERATURE AND PRESSURE EQUAL VOLUMES OF ALL GASES CONTAIN EQUAL NUMBERS OF MOLECULES.
* * AVOGADRO'S LAW * *

Try and think of the reason for this. The answer is given in Mole 5 Solutions at the end of the book.

At room temperature and pressure (RTP) one mole of any gas has a volume of 24 litres.

15

Scientists can be awkward!

The scientific unit for volume is the decimetre cubed (dm^3). One litre is the same as $1\ dm^3$. In $1\ dm^3$ there are 1000 centimetres cubed (cm^3).

So: $1\ dm^3 = 1\,l = 1000\ cm^3$

Now that we know that one mole of any gas at RTP has a volume of 24 l, we can easily convert gas volumes into number of moles. Remember that 24 l is equal to $24\ dm^3$.

$$\text{Number of moles} = \frac{\text{number of } dm^3 \text{ at RTP}}{24}$$

If the volume at RTP is in centimetres cubed then we change the equation to

$$\text{number of moles} = \frac{\text{number of centimetres cubed at RTP}}{24\ 000}$$

Example One

How many moles are contained in $48\ dm^3$ of ammonia at RTP?

Answer

$$\text{Number of moles} = \frac{\text{number of } dm^3 \text{ at RTP}}{24} = \frac{48^2}{24_1} = \textbf{2 moles of ammonia.}$$

Exercise 5.1

Calculate the number of moles of gas contained in the following volumes. The volumes are measured at RTP.

(a) $48\ dm^3$ of oxygen gas
(b) $12\ dm^3$ of ammonia gas
(c) $240\ cm^3$ of bromine gas
(d) $96\ cm^3$ of neon gas
(e) $2.4\ dm^3$ of hydrogen gas

Example Two

(Now it gets tricky!)

Find the volume in decimetres cubed at RTP of 0.2 g of hydrogen gas. [A_r(H) = 1]

Answer

Firstly we need to work out the relative molecular mass of hydrogen gas, H_2.

$2 \times 1 = 2$

Now we need to find out how many moles there are in 0.2 g of H_2.

$$\text{Number of moles} = \frac{\text{mass of gas}}{\text{relative molecular mass}} = \frac{0.2^1}{2^1} = \textbf{0.1 moles}.$$

Easy so far? Finally we use the equation we have learned in this unit.

$$\text{Number of moles} = \frac{\text{number of decimetres cubed at RTP}}{24}.$$

We rearrange it:

number of decimetres cubed at RTP = number of moles $\times$ 24

number of decimetres cubed at RTP = $0.1 \times 24 = \textbf{2.4 dm}^3$.

Exercise 5.2

Relative atomic masses you need are on the right-hand side.

Find the volume at RTP of

(a) 0.2 g of helium gas in centimetres cubed,
(b) 7.0 g of nitrogen gas, N_2, in decimetres cubed,
(c) 1.7 g of ammonia gas, NH_3, in decimetres cubed,
(d) 2.0 g of neon in decimetres cubed,
(e) 0.16 g of methane, CH_4, in centimetres cubed.

Relative atomic masses

C	=	12
H	=	1
He	=	4
N	=	14
Ne	=	20

Fight off the brain strain. Now tackle the problem in Example Three!

Example Three

What is the mass at RTP of 2.4 dm^3 of oxygen gas, O_2? [$A_r(O) = 16$]

Answer

Firstly we need to convert 2.4 dm^3 of oxygen into moles. At RTP we know that for any gas:

$$\text{number of moles} = \frac{\text{volume in decimetres cubed}}{24}.$$

So in this case, number of moles of oxygen $= \dfrac{2.4}{24} = 0.1$ moles.

Now we can find the relative molecular mass of oxygen $= 2 \times 16 = 32$.
Finally we can use 0.1 mole and relative molecular mass 32 to find the mass of oxygen gas.

$$\text{Number of moles} = \frac{\text{mass}}{\text{relative molecular mass}}.$$

So, rearranging we get

mass = number of moles $\times$ relative molecular mass
$= 0.1 \times 32 = $ **3.2 g**.

Exercise 5.3

What is the mass, at RTP, of

(a) 4 dm^3 of ammonia gas, NH_3,
(b) 2.4 dm^3 of hydrogen gas, H_2,
(c) 240 cm^3 of helium gas (careful!),
(d) 4.8 dm^3 of oxygen gas, O_2,
(e) 1.2 dm^3 of carbon dioxide gas, CO_2?

Relative atomic masses	
C	= 12
H	= 1
He	= 4
N	= 14
O	= 16

What we have learned in

MOLE 5

(1) It is easy to measure the volume of a gas.
(2) Avogadro's Law: One mole of **any** gas at the same temperature and pressure has the same volume.
(3) At room temperature and pressure, RTP, one mole of any gas has a volume of 24 dm^3.
(4) We can convert volumes into moles by using

$$\text{number of moles} = \frac{\text{number of dm}^3 \text{ at RTP}}{24}.$$

Molehill Productions Present . . .

MOLE 6 HOW MUCH HAVE I LEARNED . . . SO FAR?

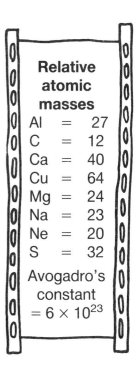

We have learned quite a lot about the mole. Have a go at the questions which follow. Show your calculations clearly. All the relative atomic masses and other information you will need are given at the side.

Exercise 6.1

What is the mass of

(a) ½ mole of magnesium atoms,
(b) 3 moles of calcium atoms,
(c) 2 moles of copper atoms?

Exercise 6.2

How many atoms are there in

(a) 20 g of neon,   (b) 24 g of carbon,
(c) 11.5 g of sodium?

Exercise 6.3

How many moles of atoms are there in

(a) 8 g of calcium,   (b) 3.2 g of sulphur,
(c) 135 g of aluminium?

Exercise 6.4

What mass of magnesium contains 2×10^{23} atoms?

Exercise 6.5

What mass of magnesium contains five times as many atoms as 2 g of carbon?

No problems so far? Again the data you need is on the right-hand side.

Relative atomic masses

Al	=	27
C	=	12
Ca	=	40
Cu	=	64
Mg	=	24
Na	=	23
Ne	=	20
S	=	32

Avogadro's constant
$= 6 \times 10^{23}$

Exercise 6.6

Find the number of moles, at RTP, of

(a) ammonia in 240 cm^3 of gas,
(b) steam in 120 cm^3 of gas,
(c) chlorine in 480 cm^3 of gas.

Exercise 6.7

Find the relative molecular mass of

(a) copper(II) carbonate, $CuCO_3$,
(b) potassium manganate(VII), $KMnO_4$
(c) aluminium hydroxide, $Al(OH)_3$,
(d) hydrated copper(II) sulphate, $CuSO_4.5H_2O$.

Exercise 6.8

Find the volume, at RTP, of

(a) 14 g of nitrogen gas, N_2 (in decimetres cubed),
(b) 1.7 g of ammonia gas, NH_3 (in decimetres cubed),
(c) 4 g of oxygen, O_2 (in centimetres cubed).

Exercise 6.9

What is the mass, at RTP, of

(a) 24 000 cm^3 of ammonia gas, NH_3,
(b) 2.4 dm^3 of oxygen gas, O_2,
(c) 1.2 dm^3 of hydrogen gas, H_2?

Relative atomic masses
Al = 27
C = 12
Cl = 35.5
Cu = 64
H = 1
K = 39
Mn = 55
N = 14
O = 16
S = 32

1 mole of any gas, at RTP, has a volume of 24 dm^3.

MOLE 7 SOLUTIONS

Often scientists carry out experiments where the chemicals involved are dissolved in water. A scientist must be able to work out how much of a substance is dissolved in a certain volume of solution. Once she knows how much is dissolved she can learn a lot more about the chemical reaction.

In Mole 5 we learned that scientists measured volumes in **decimetres cubed (dm³). One decimetre cubed is the same as one litre. One decimetre cubed can be divided up into 1000 centimetres cubed (cm³).**

The best way of understanding how much substance is dissolved in a certain volume of solution is to know its **concentration.**

If a scientist dissolves one mole of solute in enough water to make 1 dm³ of solution, then the concentration of the solution is one mole per decimetre cubed.

A concentration of **one mole per decimetre cubed** is often written as **1 mole/dm³.**

A solution which contains **2 moles** in every **dm³** of solution would have a **concentration of 2 moles/dm³.**

A solution of concentration **0.1 mole/dm³** would have **0.1 moles of solute dissoved in 1 dm³** of solution.

OK so far?

Let us imagine that a scientist wants to make a solution of sodium chloride of concentration **1 mole/dm³.** She needs to weigh out **1 mole** of sodium chloride and dissolve it in enough water to make **1 dm³** of solution.

The relative atomic mass of sodium is 23 and the relative atomic mass of chlorine is 35.5. The formula of sodium chloride is **NaCl**. So 1 mole of NaCl has a mass of $23 + 35.5 = 58.5$ g.

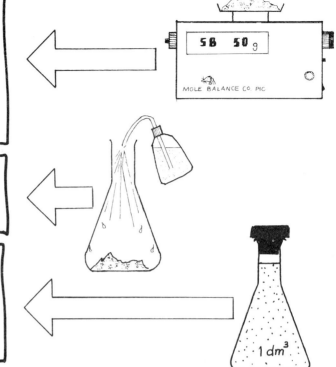

The 58.5 g of solid is carefully washed into a special 1 dm^3 graduated flask.

Water is then added and the flask is shaken. Finally water is added again until there is exactly 1 dm^3 of solution.

That is quite straightforward. Unfortunately scientists do **not** often want to make exactly 1 dm^3 of a solution of concentration 1 mole/dm^3!

For example, what if 200 cm^3 of a sodium chloride solution of concentration 0.5 mole/dm^3 is required? We need **two** equations. The first we have already met:

$$\text{number of moles} = \frac{\text{mass}}{\text{relative molecular mass}}.$$

Now we need to learn a new equation:

number of moles dissolved =
        volume in dm^3 × concentration in moles/dm^3.

Learn this

Example

What is the mass of sodium chloride needed to make 200 cm^3 of sodium chloride solution of concentration 0.5 mole/dm^3?
[A_r(Na) = 23; A_r(Cl) = 35.5]

Answer

The relative molecular mass of sodium chloride, NaCl, as we have already calculated is $23 + 35.5 = 58.5$.

The number of moles dissolved in 200 cm^3 of solution of concentration 0.5 mole/dm^3 is

number of moles dissolved = volumes in dm^3 × concentration in moles/dm^3.

Since there are 1000 cm^3 in 1 dm^3, then 200 cm^3 is 200/1000 of a dm^3. So,

number of moles dissolved = $\dfrac{200}{1000}$ × 0.5 = **0.1 mole**.

Now we can calculate the actual mass of sodium chloride needed by rearranging

number of moles = $\dfrac{\text{mass}}{\text{relative molecular mass}}$

to give

mass = number of moles × relative molecular mass.

Therefore   mass = 0.1 × 58.5 = **5.85 g**.

So to make 200 cm^3 of a solution of concentration 0.5 mole/dm^3 we would need **5.85 g** of sodium chloride.

Exercise 7.1

(a) Calculate the mass of calcium chloride, CaCl$_2$, needed to make 100 cm^3 of a solution of concentration 2 moles/dm^3.

(b) Work out the mass of pure sulphuric acid, H$_2$SO$_4$, needed to make 500 cm^3 of a solution of concentration 5 moles/dm^3.

Now put your thinking cap on!

(c) If 10.3 g of sodium bromide, NaBr, was dissolved in 250 cm^3 of solution, what would be the concentration of the solution in moles/dm^3?

(d) If 8 g of copper(II) sulphate, CuSO$_4$, was dissolved to make 500 cm^3 of solution, what would be the concentration of the solution in moles/dm^3?

Relative atomic masses	
Br	= 80
Ca	= 40
Cl	= 35.5
Cu	= 64
H	= 1
Na	= 23
O	= 16
S	= 32

What we have learned in

MOLE 7

(1) Scientists often carry out reactions in aqueous solution.
(2) It is convenient to measure the concentrations of solutions in moles/dm^3.
(3) To calculate the number of moles dissolved in a solution we use the equation:

number of moles dissolved = volume in dm^3 × concentration in moles/dm^3.

MOLE 8

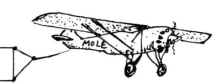

EQUATIONS

Magnesium and sulphur react together to form magnesium sulphide. We can write

magnesium + sulphur → magnesium sulphide.

This is a **word equation**. It tells us that magnesium and sulphur are the **reactants** and that magnesium sulphide is the **product**. A word equation does not tell us anything about the **proportions** in which magnesium and sulphur react.

The formula of magnesium sulphide is MgS. This tells us that magnesium and sulphur combine together in the ratio one mole of magnesium to one mole of sulphur.

> **State symbols**
> (s)   means solid
> (l)   means liquid
> (g)   means gas
> (aq) means the substance was dissolved in water (aqueous)

We can write Mg + S → MgS.
Or putting in the **state symbols** Mg(s) + S(s) → MgS(s).

This is an example of a **symbol equation**. It reads:

'One mole of magnesium atoms in the solid state reacts with one mole of sulphur atoms in the solid state to produce one mole of magnesium sulphide molecules in the solid state.'

A full symbol equation tells us

(1)   which substances are the reactants and which are the products,
(2)   the formulae of all the substances involved in the reaction,
(3)   the numbers of moles of all the substances involved,
(4)   the states of all the substances.

A symbol equation can **only** be written when the formulae of all the substances and the quantities of them involved in the reaction have been worked out **from experimental results**. A lot of experimental work is needed. Really an equation is just a summary of a lot of experiments.

An equation put forward without any experimental backing can be valueless. For example we could write an equation for the reaction between carbon and chlorine that looks sound:

$$C(s) + 2Cl_2(g) \rightarrow CCl_4(l).$$

All the formulae are correct and so are the state symbols. The equation is **balanced** – that is we have the same number of atoms on both sides. The only problem is carbon does **not** react with chlorine so the equation is worthless!

Exercise 8.1

For each of the following put into **words** the information given by the symbol equation. Do **not** just write the word equation.

(a) $2K(s) + 2H_2O(l) \rightarrow 2KOH(aq) + H_2(g)$

(b) $N_2(g) + 3H_2(g) \rightarrow 2NH_3(g)$

(c) $\begin{matrix} CuO(s) \\ \begin{bmatrix} copper(II) \\ oxide \end{bmatrix} \end{matrix} + 2HCl(aq) \rightarrow CuCl_2(aq) + H_2O(l)$ [care!]

(d) $Fe_2O_3(s) + 3CO(g) \rightarrow 2Fe(l) + 3CO_2(g)$
$\begin{bmatrix} iron(III) \\ oxide \end{bmatrix}$

(e) $2CuO(NO_3)_2(s) \rightarrow 2CuO(s) + 4NO_2(g) + O_2$
$\begin{bmatrix} copper(II) \\ nitrate \end{bmatrix}$

Note: In a balanced symbol equation the formulae always stay the same. The number of atoms on each side of the equation are balanced by **adjusting the number of moles of chemicals**.

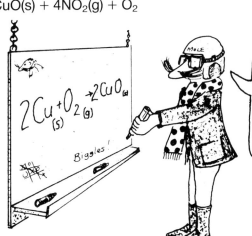

Exercise 8.2

Write out the following equations. **Balance** them by adjusting the number of **moles** of chemicals. Remember you must **not** alter the formulae.

Example

$$Fe(s) + HCl(aq) \rightarrow FeCl_2(aq) + H_2(g)$$

Answer

$$Fe(s) + 2HCl(aq) \rightarrow FeCl_2(aq) + H_2(g)$$

(a) $CaO(s) + HNO_3(aq) \rightarrow Ca(NO_3)_2(aq) + H_2O(l)$

(b) $MgCO_3(s) + HCl(aq) \rightarrow MgCl_2(aq) + CO_2(g) + H_2O(l)$

(c) $Fe(s) + Cl_2(g) \rightarrow FeCl_3(s)$

(d) $Na(s) + H_2O(l) \rightarrow NaOH(aq) + H_2(g)$

What we have learned in

MOLE 8

(1) A word equation can only tell us the reactants and products in a chemical reaction.
(2) A symbol equation can only be written if the reaction has been proved experimentally.
(3) A symbol equation gives much more information than a word equation.
(4) A symbol equation must be carefully balanced by adjusting the number of moles, not the formulae of the chemicals involved.

MOLE 9

LEARNING MORE ABOUT EQUATIONS

We have learned that a symbol equation
can be put into words to help explain what is going on.

For example

$$3CuO(s) + 2NH_3(g) \rightarrow 3Cu(s) + 3H_2O(g) + N_2(g)$$

reads 'three moles of copper(II) oxide in solid form react with two
moles of ammonia gas molecules to form three moles of copper
atoms in solid form, plus three moles of steam molecules and one
mole of gaseous nitrogen molecules.'

In Mole 4, yobbo mole showed us how to work out the mass of one
mole of a compound. Let us calculate the mass of one mole of
everything in the above equation. Then we will multiply each mass
by the number of moles in the equation.

So,

$3CuO = (64 + 16) \times 3 =$ **240 g**; $2NH_3 = (14 + 3) \times 2 =$ **34 g**;

$3Cu = (64 \times 3) =$ **192 g**; $3H_2O = (2 + 16) \times 3 =$ **54 g**;

$N_2 = (2 \times 14) =$ **28 g**.

$$3CuO(s) + 2NH_3(g) \rightarrow 3Cu(s) + 3H_2O(g) + N_2(g)$$

$$\underline{240\,g \quad + \quad 34\,g} \qquad \underline{192\,g \ + \ 54\,g \ + \ 28\,g}$$
$$= 274\,g^* \qquad\qquad = 274\,g^*$$

We can now say that 240 g of copper(II) oxide will react with 34 g
of ammonia to produce 192 g of copper, 54 g of steam and 28 g of
nitrogen.

***Note** that the masses on the left and right sides are equal. Atoms
can neither be created nor destroyed, only rearranged.

When a scientist is performing an experiment she often has to use
small quantities of chemicals. A balanced symbol equation can tell
her how much **product she should make**.

Example One

Magnesium burns in air to make magnesium oxide.

$$2\,Mg(s) + O_2(g) \rightarrow 2MgO(s)$$

What mass of magnesium oxide would be formed if 6 g of magnesium was burned in plenty (excess) of oxygen.
$[A_r(Mg) = 24; A_r(O) = 16]$

Answer

First circle what **we know** (6 g of magnesium) and what **we want to know** (? g of magnesium oxide) on the equation:

$$\text{2Mg}(s) + O_2(g) \rightarrow \text{2MgO}(s).$$

Now make a shortened version of the equation:

$$2Mg \rightarrow 2MgO.$$

Turn this shortened equation into masses:

$$2Mg = 2 \times 24 = 48\text{ g}; 2MgO = 2 \times 40 = 80\text{ g}$$

$$2Mg \rightarrow 2MgO$$
$$48\text{ g} \rightarrow 80\text{ g}$$

Hence 48 g of magnesium will make 80 g of magnesium oxide.

So   1 g of magnesium will make $\dfrac{80}{48}$ g of magnesium oxide.

And   6 g of magnesium will make $\dfrac{80}{48} \times 6$ g of magnesium oxide.

$$= \textbf{10 g}\text{ of magnesium oxide.}$$

Exercise 9.1

Calcium cyanamide, $CaCN_2$, reacts with water:

$$CaCN_2(s) + 3H_2O(l) \rightarrow CaCO_3(s) + 2NH_3(g).$$

What mass of calcium carbonate will be formed if 20 g of calcium cyanamide reacts with excess water?
$[A_r(Ca) = 40; A_r(C) = 12; A_r(N) = 14; A_r(O) = 16]$

A symbol equation can also tell a scientist how much **she needs to start with** if she wants to make a certain amount of product.

Example Two

Let us use again $2Mg(s) + O_2(g) \rightarrow 2MgO(s)$

How much magnesium is needed to make 55 g of magnesium oxide?
($A_r(Mg) = 24$; $A_r(O) = 16$.
So $2Mg = 48$ g and $2MgO = 80$ g.)

Answer

Again circle what **we know** and what **we want to know**.

Make our shortened equation: $2\,Mg \rightarrow 2MgO$
$$48\,g \rightarrow 80\,g.$$

Hence 48 g of magnesium will make 80 g of magnesium oxide.

Now $\frac{48}{80}$ g of magnesium will make 1 g of magnesium oxide.

So $55 \times \frac{48}{80}$ g of magnesium will make 55 g of magnesium oxide.

Therefore **33 g** of magnesium are needed to make 55 g of magnesium oxide.

Exercise 9.2

Copper(II) oxide reacts with hydrogen:

$$CuO(s) + H_2(g) \rightarrow Cu(s) + H_2O(g).$$

What mass of copper(II) oxide will react with excess hydrogen to produce 8 g of copper metal?
[$A_r(Cu) = 64$; $A_r(O) = 16$]

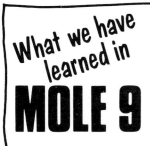 **What we have learned in MOLE 9**

(1) A symbol equation can be used by a scientist to tell her how much product she should make.
(2) A symbol equation can also be used to tell a scientist how much to start with if she needs to make a certain amount of product.

MOLE 10 CALCULATING THE PERCENTAGES OF ELEMENTS IN A COMPOUND

Scientists often want to find the **percentage of an element** in a compound. Usually this is to find out which compounds are better value for money.

Example One

What is the percentage by mass of nitrogen in ammonium sulphate, $(NH_4)_2SO_4$?
[$A_r(H) = 1$; $A_r(N) = 14$; $A_r(O) = 16$; $A_r(S) = 32$]

Answer

This is a common problem, because nitrogen is an important constituent of fertilisers.
Firstly calculate the **relative molecular mass** of ammonium sulphate:

$(NH_4)_2SO_4 = (2 \times 14) + (8 \times 1) + 32 + (4 \times 16) = 132$:
one mole = 132 g.

Now work out the mass of **nitrogen** in this compound:
Nitrogen in $(NH_4)_2SO_4 = 14 \times 2 = 28$: in one mole there would be **28 g**.

So 28 g of the 132 g are nitrogen, $\dfrac{28}{132}$ g.

As a percentage this fraction becomes $\dfrac{28}{132} \times 100 = \textbf{21.2\%}$.

Hence the percentage of nitrogen in ammonium sulphate is **21.2%**.

Example Two

Find the mass of nitrogen in 660 tonnes (t) of ammonium sulphate.

Answer

We have already calculated that 21.2% of ammonium sulphate is nitrogen. So 21.2% of the 660 t will be nitrogen:

$$\frac{21.2}{100} \times 660 = \mathbf{140\,t}.$$

Exercise 10.1

The relative atomic masses you need are on the right-hand side.

A chemical engineer has 50 t of haematite, Fe_2O_3, and 50 t of magnetite, Fe_3O_4. Which of the two ores contains the more iron?

Exercise 10.2

(a) What is the percentage of nitrogen in ammonium nitrate, NH_4NO_3?
(b) How many kilograms of nitrogen are there in 650 kg of ammonium nitrate?

Exercise 10.3

Which contains the more calcium: 450 t of calcium nitrate, $Ca(NO_3)_2$, or 400 t of calcium sulphate, $CaSO_4$?

Now for the creep point question!

Exercise 10.4

What is the mass of carbon in 48 dm^3 of methane, CH_4 at RTP?

Relative atomic masses		
C	=	12
Ca	=	40
Fe	=	56
H	=	1
N	=	14
O	=	16
S	=	32

What we have learned in

MOLE 10

(1) Scientists often want to calculate the percentage of an element in a compound.
(2) Knowing the percentage of an element in a compound helps in working out which compound is better value for money.
(3) To calculate the percentage of an element in a compound, we firstly work out the relative molecular mass of the compound. Then we find out the mass of the element in one mole of the compound. Finally,

$$\frac{\text{mass of the element in one mole of the compound}}{\text{relative molecular mass}} \times 100$$

tells us the percentage of the element.

MOLE 11 USING CONCENTRATIONS

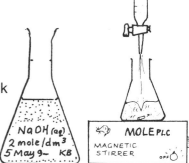

In Mole 7 we learned that

> If a scientist dissolves one mole of a solute in enough water to make 1 dm³ of solution, then the concentration of the solution is 1 mole/dm³.

Now that we have learned quite a lot about equations, we can link equations and concentrations together.

A common case is where an **acid** and a **base** are reacting together.

Example One

Put the following equation into words

$$KOH(aq) + HCl(aq) \rightarrow KCl(aq) + H_2O(l).$$

Answer

One mole of aqueous potassium hydroxide reacts with one mole of aqueous hydrochloric acid to produce one mole of aqueous potassium chloride and one more of water.

For any neutralisation reaction we can write six quantitites.

(1) The number of moles of **A**cid reacting, according to the equation: let us call this **A**.
(2) The number of moles of **B**ase reacting, according to the equation: let us call this **B**.
(3) The **C**oncentration of the acid, in moles/dm³: let us call this **Ca**.
(4) The **C**oncentration of the **b**ase, in moles/dm³: let us call this **Cb**.
(5) The **V**olume of the acid: let us call this **Va**.
(6) The **V**olume of the base: let us call this **Vb**.

Now, if we have a balanced chemical equation then

$$\mathbf{B \times Va \times Ca = A \times Vb \times Cb}.$$

Doubtful eh? OK, let's try this equation out.

PHEW*!*

Example Two

What volume of sodium hydroxide solution of concentration 2 moles/dm^3 will be needed to exactly neutralise 20 cm^3 of dilute sulphuric acid of concentration 1 mole/dm^3? The equation is:

$$2NaOH(aq) + H_2SO_4(aq) \rightarrow Na_2SO_4(aq) + 2H_2O(l)$$

Answer

Moles of acid, **A** = 1; moles of base, **B** = 2, **Va** = 20 cm^3; **Vb** = ? cm^3; **Ca** = 1 mole/dm^3; **Cb** = 2 moles/dm^3. If you cannot see where the values of **A** and **B** came from, read the equation for the reaction out loud. Also note that since **Va** is in cm^3, then our answer, **Vb** will also be in cm^3.

$$\boxed{\textbf{B} \times \textbf{Va} \times \textbf{Ca} = \textbf{A} \times \textbf{Vb} \times \textbf{Cb}}$$ Learn this

So,

$$2 \times 20 \times 1 = 1 \times \textbf{Vb} \times 2 \qquad \textbf{Vb} = 20 \text{ cm}^3.$$

The volume of sodium hydroxide required is **20 cm^3**.

Exercise 11.1

Use these equations to answer the following questions:

   (i) $NaOH(aq) + HNO_3(aq) \rightarrow NaNO_3(aq) + H_2O(l)$.
  (ii) $2KOH(aq) + H_2SO_4(aq) \rightarrow K_2SO_4(aq) + 2H_2O(l)$.

(a) Put equation (i) into words.
(b) Put equation (ii) into words.
(c) Calculate the volume of sodium hydroxide solution of concentration 1 mole/dm^3 which exactly neutralises 100 cm^3 of nitric acid of concentration 0.5 mole/dm^3.
(d) Calculate the volume of sulphuric acid of concentration 0.2 mole/dm^3 needed to exactly neutralise 25 cm^3 of potassium hydroxide solution of concentration 0.5 mole/dm^3.

What we have learned in
MOLE 11

(1) Scientists can link equations and concentration together.
(2) If we are looking at acids and bases then we use the equation:

$$\text{B} \times \text{Va} \times \text{Ca} = \text{A} \times \text{Vb} \times \text{Cb}.$$

(3) The equation above means that we can calculate volumes and concentrations if we know the equation for the reaction.

MOLE 12 HOW WELL HAVE I DONE? – PART ONE

A MESSAGE FROM ROCKER MOLE

'At the beginning of this small book you probably would not have had any idea of how to tackle the problems in MOLE 12.

See how you do. Any information you need is on the right-hand side.'

HI FANS!

12.1 Find the relative molecular mass of
(a) nitric acid, HNO_3,
(b) ammonium chloride, NH_4Cl,
(c) sodium thiosulphate, $Na_2S_2O_3$,
(d) calcium nitrate, $Ca(NO_3)_2$.

12.2 What is the mass of
(a) 2 moles of calcium atoms,
(b) ½ mole of sulphur atoms,
(c) 0.75 mole of magnesium atoms?

12.3 How many atoms are there in
(a) 20 g of calcium,
(b) 48 g of magnesium,
(c) 8 g of sulphur?

12.4 What is the mass of
(a) 2 moles of water, H_2O,
(b) 0.5 mole of hydrated copper(II) sulphate, $CuSO_4.5H_2O$,
(c) 0.75 mole of potassium manganate(VII), $KMnO_4$?

12.5 Find the number of moles (at RTP) of
(a) ammonia in 48 dm^3 of gas,
(b) chlorine in 120 cm^3 of gas,
(c) hydrogen chloride in 2.4 dm^3 of gas.

Relative atomic masses	
Ca	= 40
Cl	= 35.5
Cu	= 64
H	= 1
K	= 39
Mg	= 24
Mn	= 55
N	= 14
Na	= 23
O	= 16
S	= 32

Avogadro's Number
$= 6 \times 10^{23}$

12.6 Find the volume (at RTP) of

(a) 0.4 g of hydrogen gas, H_2 (in centimetres cubed),

(b) 3.4 g of ammonia gas, NH_3 (in decimetres cubed),

(c) 0.16 g of methane gas, CH_4 (in decimetres cubed).

12.7 Calculate the mass of iron(II) sulphate, $FeSO_4$, needed to make 500 cm^3 of a solution of concentration 2 moles/dm^3.

12.8 7.45 g of potassium chloride, KCl, was dissolved in enough water to make 250 cm^3 of solution. What is the concentration of the solution in moles/dm^3?

12.9 Put into words the information given in the symbol equation below. Remember to use the modern way of naming compounds, e.g. iron(II) oxide.

$$FeO(s) + 2HNO_3(aq) \rightarrow Fe(NO_3)_2(aq) + H_2O(l)$$

12.10 Iron reacts with steam according to the equation:

$$3Fe(s) + 4H_2O(g) \rightarrow Fe_3O_4(s) + 4H_2(g).$$

What mass of triiron tetroxide, Fe_3O_4, will be formed by the complete reaction of 1.68 g of iron?

12.11 Which contains more nitrogen: 60 g of urea, $(NH_2)_2CO$, or 100 g of ammonium sulphate, $(NH_4)_2SO_4$?

12.12 Potassium hydroxide reacts with sulphuric acid as shown by the equation:

$$2KOH(aq) + H_2SO_4(aq) \rightarrow K_2SO_4(aq) + 2H_2O(aq).$$

What volume of potassium hydroxide solution of concentration 0.5 mole/dm^3 will react exactly with 50 cm^3 of dilute sulphuric acid of concentration 2 moles/dm^3?

Relative atomic masses

C	=	12
Cl	=	35.5
H	=	1
K	=	39
Fe	=	56
N	=	14
O	=	16
S	=	32

One mole of any gas at RTP has a volume of 24 dm^3

MOLE 13 THE FINAL TEST or HOW WELL HAVE I DONE? – PART TWO

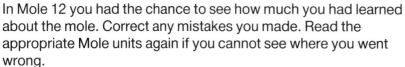

In Mole 12 you had the chance to see how much you had learned about the mole. Correct any mistakes you made. Read the appropriate Mole units again if you cannot see where you went wrong.

Now for the big one!

All the relative atomic masses and other data you need are on the right-hand side.

13.1 Find the relative molecular mass of
 (a) sulphuric acid, H_2SO_4,
 (b) ammonium sulphate, $(NH_4)_2SO_4$,
 (c) hydrated copper(II) sulphate, $CuSO_4.5H_2O$.

13.2 What is the mass of
 (a) 2 moles of magnesium atoms,
 (b) ½ mole of copper atoms,
 (c) 0.75 mole of calcium atoms?

13.3 How many atoms are there in
 (a) 1 mole of carbon atoms,
 (b) 0.5 mole of oxygen atoms,
 (c) ⅓ mole of sulphur atoms?

13.4 How many atoms are there in
 (a) 39 g of potassium,
 (b) 6.4 g of copper,
 (c) 60 g of calcium?

13.5 What is the mass of
 (a) 4 moles of water, H_2O,
 (b) 0.5 mole of sodium thiosulphate, $Na_2S_2O_3$,
 (c) 0.25 mole of ammonium dichromate, $(NH_4)_2Cr_2O_7$?

Relative atomic masses
C = 12
Ca = 40
Cr = 52
Cu = 64
H = 1
K = 39
Mg = 24
N = 14
Na = 23
O = 16
S = 32
Cl = 35.5
Avogadro's constant $= 6 \times 10^{23}$

Don't panic!

13.6 Find the number of moles, at RTP, contained in
 (a) 48 dm^3 of ammonia gas,
 (b) 240 cm^3 of nitrogen dioxide gas,
 (c) 12 dm^3 of chlorine gas.

13.7 Find the volume, at RTP, of
 (a) 0.2 g of hydrogen gas, H_2 (in centimetres cubed),
 (b) 1.7 g of ammonia gas, NH_3 (in decimetres cubed),
 (c) 0.8 g of methane gas, CH_4 (in decimetres cubed).

13.8 What is the mass (at RTP) of
(a) 240 cm³ of helium gas, He,
(b) 4.8 dm³ of hydrogen gas, H_2,
(c) 1.2 dm³ of carbon dioxide gas, CO_2?

13.9 Calculate the mass of sodium sulphate, Na_2SO_4, needed to make 500 cm³ of solution of concentration 0.5 mole/dm³.

13.10 1.03 g of sodium bromide, NaBr, was dissolved in enough water to make 250 cm³ of solution. What is the concentration of the solution in moles/dm³?

13.11 Put into words the information conveyed by the symbol equation below. Do **not** just give a word equation. Remember to use the modern naming of compounds, e.g. copper(II) chloride.

$$CuO(s) + 2HCl(aq) \rightarrow CuCl_2(aq) + H_2O(l)$$

13.12 (a) What are the percentages of nitrogen in urea, $(NH_2)_2CO$, and ammonium sulphate, $(NH_4)_2SO_4$?
(b) Which compound contains more nitrogen: 200 kg of urea, or 250 kg of ammonium sulphate?

13.13 Calcium cyanamide, $CaCN_2$, is used as a fertiliser. The following equation shows how calcium cyanamide reacts with water.

$$CaCN_2(s) + 3H_2O(l) \rightarrow CaCO_3(s) + 2NH_3(aq)$$

(a) What mass of calcium cyanamide when reacted with excess water produces 170 t of ammonia?
(b) What mass of calcium carbonate will be formed if 12.6 kg of calcium cyanamide reacts with excess water?

13.14 Sodium hydroxide reacts with sulphuric acid according to the equation:

$2NaOH(aq) + H_2SO_4(aq) \rightarrow Na_2SO_4(aq) + 2H_2O(aq).$

What volume of sodium hydroxide of concentration 0.5 mole/dm³ will react exactly with 250 cm³ of sulphuric acid of concentration 0.1 mole/dm³?

13.15 Magnesium reacts with hydrochloric acid as shown by the equation:

$$Mg(s) + 2HCl(aq) \rightarrow MgCl_2(aq) + H_2(g).$$

(a) What volume of hydrochloric acid of concentration 2 moles/dm³ reacts exactly with 0.1 mole of magnesium?
(b) What mass of hydrogen is produced when 0.1 mole of magnesium reacts with excess acid?
(c) What volume of hydrogen, at RTP, would be formed if 0.24 g of magnesium reacted with excess acid?

Relative atomic masses	
Br	= 80
C	= 12
Ca	= 40
Cl	= 35.5
Cu	= 64
H	= 1
He	= 4
N	= 14
Na	= 23
O	= 16
S	= 32
Mg	= 24

One mole of any gas at RTP has a volume of 24 dm³

37

MOLE 14 THE ANSWERS

Mole One
Exercise 1.1
(a) 4 g (b) 56 g (c) 39 g (d) 32 g
(e) 195 g (f) *119 g* (g) 127 g (h) 31 g

Exercise 1.2
(a) 6×10^{23} (b) 3×10^{23}
(c) 1.2×10^{24} or 12×10^{23} (d) 3×10^{23}
(e) 6×10^{23} (f) 3×10^{23}
(g) 1.2×10^{24} or 12×10^{23} (h) 1.5×10^{23}

Mole Two
Exercise 2.1
(a) 0.5 mole (b) 2 moles (c) 0.2 mole
(d) 2 moles (e) 0.25 mole (f) 0.1 mole
(g) 2.3 g (h) 216 g (i) 4 g (j) 448 g
(k) 1.5 g (l) 16 g

Exercise 2.2
(a) 6×10^{23} (b) 1.2×10^{24} or 12×10^{23}
(c) 3×10^{23} (d) 2×10^{23} (e) 8 g (f) 4 g
(g) 20 g (h) 13 g

Mole Three
Exercise 3.1
(a) 0.1 mole (b) 2 moles

Exercise 3.2
(a) 4 g (b) 40 g (c) 142 g

Mole Four
Exercise 4.1
(a) 80 (b) 80 (c) 96 (d) 124 (e) 189
(f) 96

Exercise 4.2
(a) 0.25 mole (b) 2.256 moles
(c) 0.75 mole (d) 0.33 mole

Exercise 4.3
(a) 50 g (b) 20 g (c) 8 g (d) 24 g

Mole Five
Avogadro's Law . . . Why? If we take one mole of any gas, we have taken exactly the same number of gas molecules. Provided the temperature and pressure are kept the same one mole of any gas will have the same volume.

Exercise 5.1
(a) 2 moles (b) 0.5 mole (c) 0.01 mole
(d) 0.004 mole (e) 0.1 mole

Exercise 5.2
(a) 1200 cm^3 (b) 6 dm^3 (c) 2.4 dm^3
(d) 2.4 dm^3 (e) 240 cm^3

Exercise 5.3
(a) 2.83 g (b) 0.2 g (c) 0.04 g (d) 6.4 g
(e) 2.2 g

Mole Six
Exercise 6.1
(a) 12 g (b) 120 g (c) 128 g

Exercise 6.2
(a) 6×10^{23} (b) 1.2×10^{24} or 12×10^{23}
(c) 3×10^{23}

Exercise 6.3
(a) 0.2 mole (b) 0.1 mole (c) 5 moles

Exercise 6.4
8 g

Exercise 6.5
20 g

Exercise 6.6
(a) 0.01 mole (b) 0.005 mole (c) 0.02 mole

Exercise 6.7
(a) 124　(b) 158　(c) 78　(d) 250

Exercise 6.8
(a) $12 \, dm^3$　(b) $2.4 \, dm^3$　(c) $3000 \, cm^3$

Exercise 6.9
(a) 17 g　(b) 3.2 g　(c) 0.1 g

Mole Seven
Exercise 7.1
(a) 22.2 g　(b) 245 g　(c) $0.4 \, mole/dm^3$
(d) $0.1 \, mole/dm^3$

Mole Eight
Exercise 8.1 (Your answers could be worded slightly differently to these.)
(a) Two moles of potassium atoms in the solid state react with two moles of water molecules in the liquid state to produce two moles of aqueous potassium hydroxide and one mole of hydrogen gas.
(b) One mole of gaseous nitrogen molecules reacts with three moles of gaseous hydrogen molecules to produce two moles of gaseous ammonia molecules.
(c) One mole of copper(II) oxide in the solid state reacts with two moles of dilute hydrochloric acid to produce one mole of aqueous copper(II) chloride and one mole of water.
(d) One mole of solid iron(III) oxide reacts with three moles of carbon monoxide molecules in the gaseous state to produce two moles of liquid iron atoms and three moles of carbon dioxide gas molecules.
(e) Two moles of copper(II) nitrate in the solid state produce two moles of copper(II) oxide in the solid state, four moles of gaseous nitrogen dioxide molecules and one mole of gaseous oxygen molecules.

Exercise 8.2
(a) $CaO(s) + 2HNO_3(aq) \rightarrow$
$$Ca(NO_3)_2(aq) + H_2O(l)$$
(b) $MgCO_3(s) + 2HCl(aq) \rightarrow$
$$MgCl_2(aq) + CO_2(g) + H_2O(l)$$
(c) $2Fe(s) + 3Cl_2(g) \rightarrow 2FeCl_3(s)$
(d) $2Na(s) + 2H_2O(l) \rightarrow 2NaOH(g) + H_2(g)$

Mole Nine
Exercise 9.1
25 g

Exercise 9.2
10 g

Mole Ten
Exercise 10.1
Magnetite contains more iron (72.4%) than haematite (70%).

Exercise 10.2
(a) 35% nitrogen　(b) 227.5 kg

Exercise 10.3
Calcium sulphate

Exercise 10.4
24 g

Mole Eleven
Exercise 11.1
(a) One mole of aqueous sodium hydroxide reacts with one mole of dilute nitric acid to produce one mole of aqueous sodium nitrate and one mole of water.
(b) Two moles of aqueous potassium hydroxide solution react with one mole of dilute sulphuric acid to produce one mole of aqueous potassium sulphate and two moles of water.
(c) $50 \, cm^3$　(d) $31.25 \, cm^3$

Mole Twelve
Exercise 12.1
(a) 63　(b) 53.5　(c) 158　(d) 164

Exercise 12.2
(a) 80 g　(b) 16 g　(c) 18 g

Exercise 12.3
(a) 3×10^{23}　(b) 1.2×10^{24}　(c) 1.5×10^{23}

Exercise 12.4
(a) 36 g　(b) 125 g　(c) 118.5 g

Exercise 12.5
(a) 2 moles   (b) 0.005 mole   (c) 0.1 mole

Exercise 12.6
(a) 4800 cm^3 (b) 4.8 dm^3 (c) 0.24 dm^3

Exercise 12.7
152 g

Exercise 12.8
0.4 mole/dm^3

Exercise 12.9
One mole of solid iron(II) oxide reacts with two moles of dilute nitric acid to produce one mole of aqueous iron(II) nitrate and one mole of water.

Exercise 12.10
2.32 g

Exercise 12.11
60 g of urea

Exercise 12.12
400 cm^3

Mole Thirteen
Exercise 13.1
(a) 98   (b) 132   (c) 250

Exercise 13.2
(a) 48 g   (b) 32 g   (c) 30 g

Exercise 13.3
(a) 6 × 10^{23} (b) 3 × 10^{23} (c) 2 × 10^{23}

Exercise 13.4
(a) 6 × 10^{23} (b) 0.6 × 10^{23} or 6 × 10^{22}
(c) 9 × 10^{23}

Exercise 13.5
(a) 72 g   (b) 79 g   (c) 63 g

Exercise 13.6
(a) 2 moles   (b) 0.01 mole   (c) 0.5 mole

Exercise 13.7
(a) 2400 cm^3 (b) 2.4 dm^3 (c) 1.2 dm^3

Exercise 13.8
(a) 0.04 g   (b) 0.4 g   (c) 2.2 g

Exercise 13.9
35.5 g

Exercise 13.10
0.04 mole/dm^3

Exercise 13.11
One mole of solid copper(II) oxide reacts with two moles of dilute hydrochloric acid to produce one mole of aqueous copper(II) chloride and one mole of water.

Exercise 13.12
(a) Urea = 46.7%, ammonium sulphate = 21.2%
(b) Urea [93.2 kg] contains more nitrogen.

Exercise 13.13
(a) 400 tonnes   (b) 15.75 kg

Exercise 13.14
(a) 100 cm^3

Exercise 13.15
(a) 100 cm^3 or 0.1 dm^3 (b) 0.2 g
(c) 240 cm^3 or 0.24 dm^3